For Jack and Anna

—M. M.

For Nigel and Annie

—A. A.

Henry Holt and Company, LLC, *Publishers since 1866*
115 West 18th Street, New York, New York 10011
www.henryholt.com

Henry Holt is a registered trademark of Henry Holt and Company, LLC
Text copyright © 2001 by Margaret Mayo. Illustrations copyright © 2001 by Alex Ayliffe
All rights reserved.
First published in the United States in 2002 by Henry Holt and Company, LLC
Originally published in England in 2001 by Orchard Books

Library of Congress Cataloging-in-Publication Data
Mayo, Margaret.
Dig dig digging / Margaret Mayo; illustrated by Alex Ayliffe.
Originally published in England in 2001 by Orchard Books.
Summary: Simple rhymes introduce various large vehicles, such as dump trucks,
fire engines, and tractors, and describe the work that they do.
1. Motor vehicles—Juvenile literature. [1. Motor vehicles.] I. Ayliffe, Alex, ill. II. Title.
TL147.M38 2002   629.225—dc21   2001002666

ISBN 0-8050-6840-6 / First American Edition—2002
Printed in Singapore
3 5 7 9 10 8 6 4

Dig Dig Digging

written by **Margaret Mayo**

illustrated by **Alex Ayliffe**

Henry Holt and Company

New York

Diggers

Diggers are good at **dig**, **dig**, **dig**ging,
scooping up the earth, and lifting and tipping.
They make huge holes with their **dig**, **dig**, **dig**ging.
They can work all day.

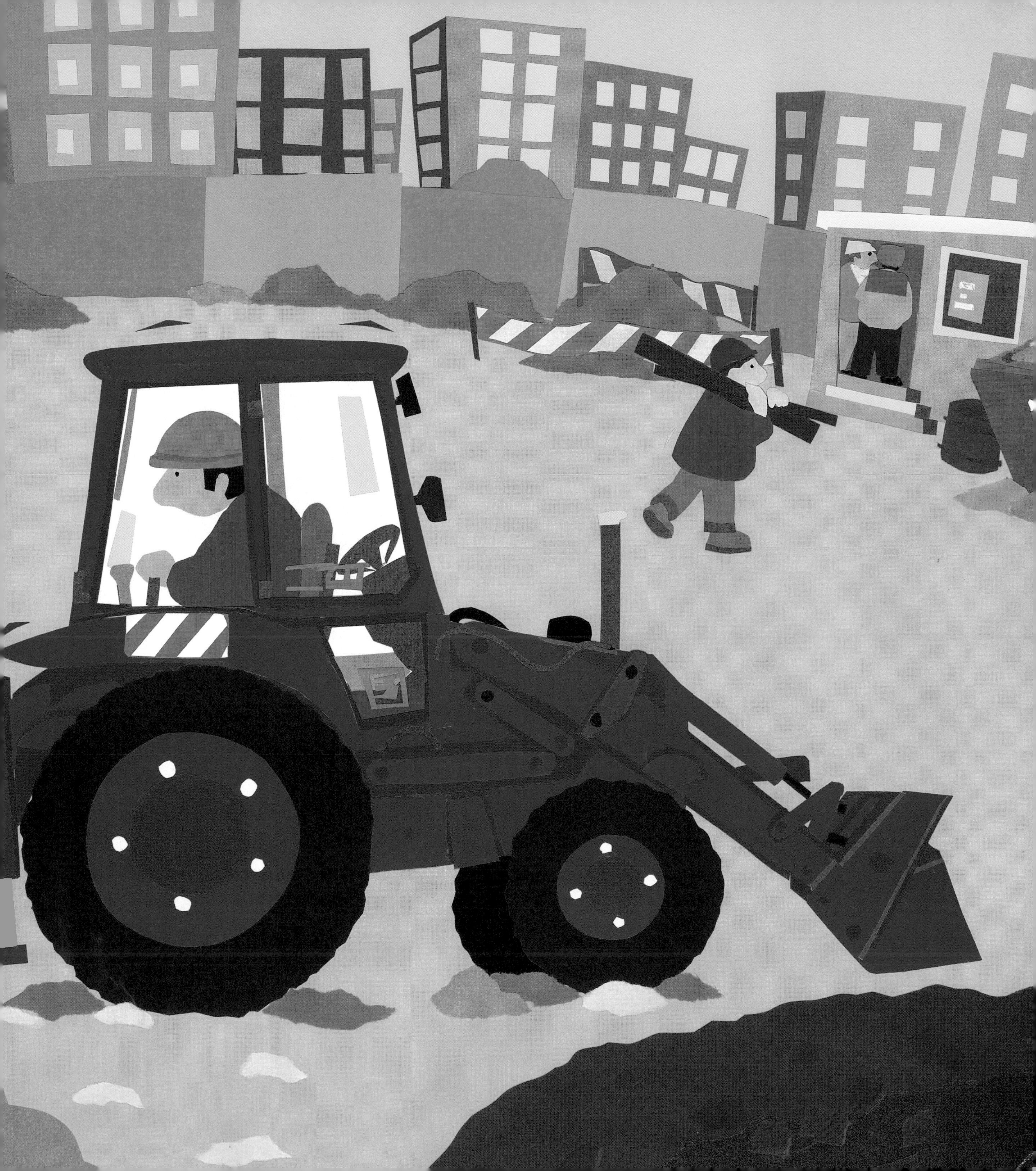

Fire Engines

Fire engines are good at race, race, racing.
Look out! Look out! Bright lights flashing.
Hoses at the ready for swoosh, swoosh, swooshing.
They can work all day.

Tractors

Tractors are good at pull, pull, pulling,
plowing up the field with a squelch, squelch, squelching.

Round go the wheels. See the dirt flying!
They can work all day.

Garbage Trucks

Garbage trucks are good at gobble, gobble, gobbling,

crunching messy garbage bags, squeezing and squashing.

Busy, busy garbage eaters, always gobbling.

They can work all day.

Cranes

Cranes are good at
lift,
lift,
lifting.
Up go the bricks
to the
top of
the building.

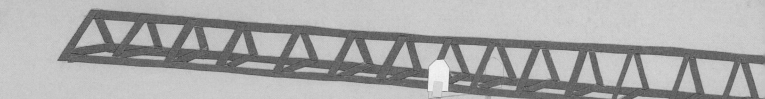

Down come the pipes,
very
slowly
spinning.
They
can
work
all day.

Transporters are good at car transporting.

Ramps down, ramps up, shiny cars loading.

All aboard! Off they go—

vroom-vroom-vrooming.

They can work all day.

Dump Trucks

Dump trucks are good at dump, dump, dumping,
carrying heavy loads, and tip, tip, tipping.
Out fall the rocks—

CRASH!

—rumbling and tumbling.
They can work all day.

Rescue Helicopters

Helicopters are good at whir, whir, whirring,
hovering and zooming, rotor blades whizzing.
Down comes the rope. Look! Someone needs rescuing!
They can work all day.

Rollers are good at roll, roll, rolling,
pressing hot, sticky tar, smoothing and spreading,
flattening the new road and slowly rolling.
They can work all day.

Bulldozers

Bulldozers are good at push, push, pushing,
over rough, bumpy ground, scraping and shoving.

Caterpillar treads are grip, grip, gripping.
They can work all day.

Trucks

Trucks are good at l o n g - d i s t a n c e traveling.
Long ones, tall ones, different loads carrying.
Blowing their horns—beep-beep!—their big wheels turning.
They can work all day.

What a busy day! Now it's time for resting.
Brakes on, engines off, the sun is setting.
No beep-beeping, no vroom-vrooming.
Shhh!
They can rest all night.